MAKES YOU STOP AND THINK

ALSO BY DANIEL HOFFMAN

MAKES YOU STOP AND THINK *Sonnets*

by DANIEL HOFFMAN

George Braziller Publishers NEW YORK

Published in 2005 by George Braziller, Inc.

Copyright © 2005 by Daniel Hoffman

For information, please address the publisher:

George Braziller

171 Madison Avenue

New York, NY 10016

Library of Congress Cataloging-in-Publication Data:

Hoffman, Daniel, 1923-
Makes you stop and think : sonnets / by Daniel Hoffman.-- 1st ed.
    p. cm.
Includes bibliographical references.
ISBN 0-8076-1561-7
1. Sonnets, American. I. Title.
PS3515.02416M35 2005
811'.54--dc22
                    2005011517

Design by Jerry Kelly
Printed and bound in the United States of America
First edition

Again, for E. McF. H.
With serendipity, as in a rhyme

CONTENTS

MAKES YOU STOP AND THINK

The Sonnet

Remembering Louise Bogan

The Sonnet, she told the crowd of bearded
        youths, their hands exploring
                rumpled girls,
                is a sacred

vessel: it takes a civilization
        to conceive its shape or know
                its uses. The kids
                stared as though

a Sphinx now spake the riddle of
        a blasted day. And few,
                she said, who would
                be *avant-garde*

consider that the term is drawn
        from tactics in the Prussian
                war, nor think
                when once they've breached

the fortress of a form, then send
        their shock-troops yet again
                to breach the form,
                there's no form—

—they asked for her opinion of
      "the poetry of Rock."
            After a drink
            with the professors

she said, This is a bad time,
      bad for poetry.
            Then with maenad
            gaze upon

the imaged ghost of a comelier day:
      I've enjoyed this visit,
            your wife's sheets
            are Irish linen.

A Legacy

Wakened by birdcalls, I stroll down our lane.
I touch the infinite sky, the barbarian sun.
I'm tousled by a breeze that smells of rain.
I do believe this day has just begun.
My legacy from History is Now:
I'll take it—in the air, in the mouth, in the dandle-bed,
In the savor, in the spending, in the *Times*, in the apple bough,
In that dream I first dreamed when I was eleven,
A stifled cry, then joy! *I am not dead!*—
For reality is vintage and delicious
Especially when you taste it while it brews
Because it comes as love comes, heart-skip sudden,
Yet long as a lifetime in a once past wishes,
A gift you couldn't have the wit to choose.

The Arrival

Odd how they burdened him though duty-free,
His Father's bags. So too, the old-time guide-
Book weighed him down. These days it seemed few tried
To puzzle its old ways, and nobody
Gabbles in that dialect in this town
That towers too high for any human need.

Yet things his Pa had said proved true indeed—
Old saws recalled too late as he strolled down
The wharf, his pockets picked, his choice defined.
Thus unencumbered, feet on solid ground,

Remembered caravels that came to find
A different land from what in fact they'd found.
Agape at topless towers, he set his mind
To reckon what he'd come to find or found.

David's Folly

The town was famous then, though few recall
When the seven Tapley brothers sailed the seas,
Each captain of a vessel named to please
A girl back here, to whom he'd tell his tall
And hair's-breadth tales of heathen, rock, and squall . . .
How many yearned for the rush of an offshore breeze,
But most stayed home, to plant and pick their peas,
Cut hay, wood, stone, ice, and haul
What they had cut: lives measured by the rod.
Their boast, how big their barns—till David Wasson
Outbuilt all with his Folly; who knew here trod
An unsung Psalmist, chores his orison,
Who scorched *The Dial* with diatribes on God
And wrote three poems that once pleased Emerson?

That Morning

You said. Not in the house, the barn, the yard—
Going on fourteen, I said, it will go hard
With him he's such a lazy shiftless lout.
High time he did his chores. I raised a shout
Flinging his name across the fields toward
The cliff. . . . only a broken echo jarred
The long silence with its stabbing doubt.

What if I hadn't when we turned to leave
The farm that morning as they pecked our corn
Said I'd give a penny for each dead crow
I thought—and ran to where the fence was torn:
A boy crossed barbed wire, pulled his shotgun through
Till trigger caught, and the years are ours to grieve.

Regrets

Bert—he was young then—ran clean out of breath
Up Backwood Mountain so as he could tell
Joe Baribeau, "Your shack's afire!" With a yell
Joe dropped his axe and raced back down the path,
Me running after, Bert behind. He crashed
Like a moose through underbrush till, at the clearing
A tree-root caught his foot. He went down swearing,
Lunged straight toward the rock his forehead smashed—

Killed him outright. Could tell that at a glance.

His shack was blazing but I made a dash—
Knew where his trousers hung. I'd find his gun.
Next day the sheriff, poking through the ruin,
In his burnt pocket found eighty bucks in cash.

Sure wish I'd knowed what Joe stashed in those pants.

Who Done It?

Who trampled down the ripe raspberry patch?
Who smashed apart the chicken coop, then fled?
Who tipped the beehives in the berry field?
Who ate the daisies? Rolled in the purple vetch?
Who left huge tracks and a black turd
Big as a turnip on the logging road?
Who's got the dogs all riled or terrified?
Who skulks in the alders by the old churchyard

While mothers crouch with children, latch and bar
Secured? The fathers boast, at Davy's Bar,
They'll bring their telescopic sights to bear . . .
How soon village decorum proves threadbare:
He points his muzzle North, where the Dipper's bare
Glints fathom a freedom he can bear.

Off Stonington

You can spot them with your naked eye
A mile off-island, sporting where Black Ledges
Jut, cavorting specks whose becks and nudges
The distance graces with pure symmetry.
As we veer near them, how voluptuously
They plunge, then ply the sullen swell that lashes
Those dour rocks. They'd tempt whoever watches
Caught in the deep gaze of the seal's eye.

Off Stonington, in oilskins, lobstermen
Who daily tread the sea but cannot swim
Know these creatures, joyous and content
In the dark swirl of their fatal element,
To be the shapes—as Monty Haskell said—
Of the living souls of fishermen drowned dead.

Sacred Things

When the mine was opened all at Perry's Store
Were of one mind. The good times would begin,
Nobody'd mind, some money coming in
Might cost the town the life it led before.

Now Goose Pond's dammed and drained, we hear no more
The reversing tidal falls. The minehead's din
Cracks the still blue sky, and trucks roll in
Where lovers used to spoon along the shore.

When their backhoe, under Cemetery Bluff
Scraped road-gravel for the mine—"No fear,
We stopped 'em when they'd gone just far enough,"

Pete took another swig of his chilled beer,
Then spat and smeared wet lips on his stained cuff—
"They better know, some things are sacred here."

Percy Gray

Born first, stayed longer in the womb,
Staked out a prior claim he'd never quit
No matter I outrasseled him. Was it
For spite he seized and locked room after room
In the mansion of her love? Each exquisite
Grace—his music, manners, that green thumb—
Made him more favored. What feat of mine could come
Between them with mere guts and mother-wit?

Now he's obliged me—I'm his only heir
And therefore hers. But what could he bequeath?
I've torn the house down, smashed his fiddle, sold
The spoons and left his grave unmarked. I swear
There's nothing I want from him but to grow old
And know his name's forgotten while I breathe.

Dr. Kilmer

Why was it, while I stared with gaping jaws
Rigid in his chair, the needled gum
Ceasing to sting, then growing thick and numb,
The mouth spread-eagled wide with rolls of gauze,
That, having drilled dead matter, in a pause
To let subside the stabs that overcome
Narcosis when a nerve's sensorium
Is pierced, he told about his brother-in-law's
Diagnosis?
    —How the doctor broke
The news one visiting hour, took him aside
To drop the word on, then just walked away;
How on the fire escape they shared a smoke
Till his brother grabbed him by the throat and cried,
"*You* wouldn't shit me, Mike—*What did he say?*"

His Own Way

Boards, nails, staples, lengths of rope
And tools were issued to them all. They toiled
In a scorch of sawdust to the hammers' yelp
Making boxes, as required: two-holed
For legs, the rig held up by shoulder-straps
And as they marched all whistled the same tune.

One there was who chafed at this till scrapes
From pine the same cut as his fellows' pine
Bruised his shinbones. Craftily, by chops
Of saw, remade his box octagonal
While walking.
             Next, from his lips a new trill sounded.
Now hopped, now strode in individual steps.
Then, as he looked about, he was surrounded
By octagons that kept his stride and whistle.

Pin-Ball

Better than motorbikes, this tensile fusion!
Nerves and body staked, exploding balls
A blinding jaggle of lights in the throbbed jungle
Where bumpers bash huge numbers and brash bells
Spin and clang to score the potent hipbone,
Measured by those digits. One could call it
Skill he leans with on the glass case, motion
Moving with the swerves of the hard pellet.
It's boredom, boredom, the incubus that's flapping
Beyond the neon in the swollen dark
While gongs flash and bells burp and flippers
Heave and heave and heave as lights bark—
The scoreboard reels as though it had been dealt
All purposed strength, this side the sign marked *TILT*.

O Sweet Woods

Down my most tangled paths of reverie
A man with a transistor radio walks.
Sweet are these woods, O solitariness;
This stranger with convivial Rock box gawks
In mine. He comes alone, strolls unbefriended,
By vibraharps' pubescent plaints attended.
Full-ON reception blurs the voice that talks.

Surfeit with speech, I'd drink in strength from silence
Anonymous in a crowd. But me he stalks,
Nor rests to skew my solitariness.
Past network's blare all his reception balks;
How could he bear the hush that I intended?
Such paucity unended must be ended—
Full-ON my reverie's assassin walks.

Violence

After I'd read my poem about a brawl
between two sidewalk hustlers—one,
insulted, throws the other down and nearly
kills him—over coffee and cookies a grave
senior citizen reproved me. *How
could you see such violence and you
didn't try to stop them?*—Oh, I explained,
it wasn't like that, really—I saw

two guys in a shoving match and thought
I'd write about aggression, what
anger really feels like. . . . *Yes,
and if the one got killed
it would be on your head.
You should've stopped them,* he said.

Ten Thousand Dreaming Seamen

Ten thousand dreaming seamen proven wrong
About the Mermaid? Researchers all agree,
They misrecalled the bearded manatee
That pouts and floats, fat lady-like, along
Southern lagoons; further, it pleased their fancy
To strum the snoutish snorts of that dugong
On memory's lyre. Such, such, "the Siren's song"
That wove her nets of fateful power.
                              Now free
They are to sail some rockbound northern coast
Where girls as sleek as seals sun on the beach;
One, at their ship's approach, slips in, swims nearer
—O sorceress whose molten eyes beseech,
Entangled in your wake, can the seafarer
Turn from your proffered love, or not be lost?

Her Gift

Her gift brings pleasure, delicately wrought,
For all she said she sang, or seemed to sing;
If she but muttered Yang she dreamed of Ying,
All oppositions beautifully brought
To the reconciliation of her thought
With disciplined decorum burnishing
Whatever it was her heart's unburdening
Gave cadence to, as though it came unsought,

Save when a chance word gouges to the quick
A hidden scar,
Or unstifleable woe

Breathes on the things no choice of hers can change,
She trembles, a windblown wick,
Her tercets shake the bars of their narrow cage.

The Hour

Soon it was over. Long, it puzzled him.
Holding in mind their strenuous delight
—How as they cleaved together they cleaved the night
To pulse through time, their twining limb with limb
Touching the pitch of a pine-torch on a tower
To split the sky with flames of its own will
Fed on the rush of their desire, until
It guttered out, after, say, a quarter-hour
And they lay still.

         Next to her tranquil face,
The breasts that held the moon's spell in their globes,
That waist, slim as a handspan, and those hips,

Why must he feel, his lips so near her lips
Who'd cast the world off with their cast-off robes,
The hour already passing without a trace?

Claims

Why had they sworn inviolable vows
But to put the world under a spell?
Remember, World, You're not to thrust pell-mell
Into their bedroom claims none could refuse
On heart or conscience—in that citadel
All's set aside for their own mutual use,
Since they are one another's, else for whose
Sakes have they made their lives inseparable?

—Not for the mothers who, still unforgiving,
Would blight their sheets with candor of the Sphinx;
Nor kids, rebellious, clinging, each conceiving
Its whims the one sole thought a parent thinks;
Nor Brother Jack, who still can't make a living
Nor Sister Jill, once beautiful, who drinks.

Miracles

For E.

Where are the scholars who can comprehend
If there's a Mind that planned the universe?
Now that we know even the farthest stars
Cannot yet touch the end—is there an end?—
Of blackness, for the fading glints they send
Toward us have travelled fourteen million years
From where they were when the gleam we see appears,
While deep and deeper in the dark they wend—

Miraculous? Not more so than the Scheme
That through infinitudes of Space, of Time
And generations brought us together, so
We'll give fulfillment to its destined Theme—
The more than life-long love that links us two
With serendipity, as in a rhyme.

Emblems

When the mandibles of the clock have gnawed
The journal of another day,
So many drawn breaths nearer
A next incarnation,

I find in that no solace.
My enterprise dissembles nature's plan.
I would hold age in stiff abeyance
And command time's watchdog to obedience

To the intensities of joy: A windy
Cloudless day of dolphins around a dory,
Beachfire, the surge, the wildness of the sea,

And the secret fissures of one woman's love
—Among the emblems I array to daunt
Too swift precessions of the moon and sun.

In That High House

In that high house half up a hill
A road coiled round the hill's stone breast.
A string linked your hand to my hand.
Our string pulls taut, frays, snaps apart.
The castle's ruined, a winter's tree.
You mustn't cry now, little son.
The rooftree's fallen and the moon
Through skeletal shadows lights the hall.
Beyond the broken door a road coils toward
A ridge where another house may stand.
And your hand loop another hand
And when that filament frays and falls
In roofless walls remember us,
When most together most alone.

Charley Hoope

He never worked, yet wore spats and received
My father on his porch. Then I would peer
Around the stoop, and all they'd say, I'd hear:
No stock but was a bull.
                  My Dad believed
All of his tips because, when Charley braved
Those shells in No-Man's Land and the snipers' fire
To drag a doughboy back from the barbed wire,
It would be a Senior Partner that he'd saved—

A loan of life still, after a decade,
Amortized by calls that named the share
Certain to rise, and an instant fortune made.

But who owed Dad the debt that Charley's words
Were to redeem? Why should his tipster care
That all our fairy gold would turn to turds?

Survivors

Through a fissure in the frozen lake
Between Siberian mountains, they could sense
Its dark shape indistinctly: some immense
Thing, a body caught trying to break
Free deep in ice. No midnight sun could wake
That hairy hump half-hidden in the glacier.

What was it? Kobold, beast, or man-like ogre?
They chipped and chopped with hammer, axe, and stake,
Until subtraction of the snow
Sculpted what had survived death of its kind

Ten thousand years. There lay the mastodon,
His meat as firm as though some rash Cro-Magnon
Had beaned him with a boulder hours ago.
On his thawed flesh, broiled over coals, they dined.

The Comanche

Weak after long fasting, felt a slow
Trembling shake the earth—the buffalo!—
And raced his pony barebacked toward the herd.
That morning not a brave in camp could gird
Himself with strength to bend the stout bowstem,
Yet with bursting arms he twangs his arrow
Deep in the bison's heart! Comanches know
The Great Spirit when it possesses them.

And now the poet, half a savage bound
By the hungers of his tribe, paces his swift
Foray across a desolate hunting-ground,
In hopes to run to earth a fleeting creature
And with the unpremeditated gift
Of spirit, seize imagination's meat.

Scrolls from the Dead

We already had some gospels, when he fell
Into a cave of potsherds and a screed
Tattered by beetles, half-unreadable.
Years to break the cipher. Who had need
Of his long, earpulled labors, all to eke
Unknown annunciations into a guise
Of English? "From golden meekness may the meek
Inherit meekness. Unfallen, the mighty rise.
Birds shall nest in the dust, and lay stones."

Why couldn't he let us go about our business,
The mighty guzzling at their bar of brass,
The meek weaned on the skimmed milk of meekness
As fewer birds return each Spring, our solace
An old tale of the breath that stirs the bones?

Lines for Scott Nearing

And what if you were wrong about Albania?
You called child labor capitalism's disease
When children worked in the coal mines of Trustees
Of the University of Pennsylvania,
Who fired you from their Wharton School forthwith—
A *cause célèbre*! Our tenured free speech grew
Out of "the Nearing Case." But not for you,
Old rebel loner, bound by reason's myth
That the just economy's completely planned.
Was this what in your old age drew the young
To your walled garden, as witness to a life
Of Thoreau's abnegations, though with a wife?
Your rows of Escarole, Romaine, Deer's Tongue—
How comely, how proportionate your land.

Old Age

When it began he was already losing
Interest in the new work by the young.
His own, like X-rays probing, undismayed,
The self whose image brands each dread decade
In lines to which the culture's climbers clung,
Had of a sudden ceased, without his choosing,
To be novel.
           Less and less inclined
Down darkness at the ends of roads to thrust
His curious, illuminating mind,
For Reality he'd take what he could trust:
The impulse of an art he couldn't stop
Reached back toward all he once by will outgrew
—Nothing so fine now, since his growing up,
No truth as telling as his youth was true.

The Sacred Fount

Stubborn hidalgo, rusting in his mail,
Outliving enemies, his loves, his time.
What spell, what doom lures him to hope that Time,
Whose breath seres every limb, would leave him hale?

The stagnant swamps he's swigged! How many's the time
Since being gulled by a Medicine Man's tall tale
He's almost found that fount, but weary, frail,
An old dog can but piddle away his time.

Who hasn't hacked through mangroves, with just his luck
Gulped potions, bottles, jugs, trying to suck
The juvenescent dew from the earth's breast

While Memory's daughter still holds out her Grail—
She sings, from thickets serried as chain-mail,
One taste, and a body is forever blessed.

Philosophy

In sophomore year the great philosopher,
Then ninety, out of retirement came, to pass
His wisdom on to one more generation.
Reading his last lecture to our class,

That afternoon the mote-filled sunlight leaned
Attentively with purpose through the tall
Windows in amber buttresses that seemed
To gird the heavens so they wouldn't fall.

The blaze of his white mane, his hooded eyes,
The voice that plumbed us from reflection's skies
So far above temptation or reward—

The scene has never left my mind. I wrote
His lecture down, but, in an old trunk, my notes
Have crumbled, and I can't recall a word.

A Resurrection

When I arose I knew I had been dead.
My fingers and my lungs still grey with clay,
Before my eyes a gleaming world unrolled,
Behind, the dark curled deeper in its cell.

What cold grip clutched my back? Mouldy breath
At each gulp clearer, warmer . . . I am forgetting
The long impenetrableness of death
Beyond remembrance and past all forgetting.

Coffee! O.J.! Let this day be a boon!
In clarifying light, in freshening weather
Memory revives—the future is its gift

While shadows of tall clocks shrivel in the sun.
I'll plunge into the maelstrom of our swift
Redemptive life, for there may be no other.

A Secret

Why, listening to London's sounds,
Does this one thought insistently recur—
In all, our numbers total scarcely more
Than a headcount of the dwellers in this town.

In the nation's capital one feels the pull
Of ties that tug him toward five continents.
A guest here, I am treated well. Content,
I could relax, as in a spa's warm pool.

But what can all these people know of me?
If they were angels, even, how to them
Would our strange, unrelated tongue make sense,

And could they peer deep in our hearts to see
Our secret? Here, my life's significance
Is this: Hungarian is what I am.

[*István Vas*]

At the Grave of Countess Potocka

[Who, captured by Tartars,
was held in a harem]

In Spring's dominion, under the orange trees
You withered, lissome rose, as long-past days,
Diminishing like butterflies on a sun-gold haze,
Blighted your heart with cocoons of memories.

Toward Poland, down those distant northern skies,
Why do such swarms of stars the way still blaze?
Did they snatch fire from that unceasing gaze
That burned the heavens with the longing in your eyes?

O Polish beauty, I'll die in exile too—
Let kind hands cast this earth upon me then,
And when the travellers pause, and speak of you,

I'll wake from sleep to hear our own dear tongue . . .
May he who sings your sorrows to life again
Seeing my grave near, make my griefs too his song.

[Adam Mickiewicz]

The Disinherited

I am the unconsoled, the widowed one,
The Prince of Aquitaine whose tower is ruined;
My only *Star* is dead, my lute, attuned
To the Heavens, bears Melancholy's crepe-black sun.

You, in the midnight of the tomb my solace,
Give back Posillipo, the Italian sea,
The *Flower* that in my grief helped to assuage me,
And the arbor where the rose and grape embrace . . .

Am I Eros, Apollo, or Biron?
The queen's kiss has left my cheek afire,
I've dreamed in the grotto where the siren swims . . .

And twice, in triumph, have crossed Acheron
And alternately pluck on Orpheus' lyre
The sighings of the saint, the nymph's wild hymns.

[*Gérard de Nerval*]

Parsifal

He has repulsed the alluring persiflage
Of girls half giddy with desire, repressed
His virginal yen to feel a yielding breast
Or rise to a temptress' teasing badinage,

He has rebuffed the Woman of subtile charms
Despite her décolletage's sly enticement,
It's Hell he's conquered, and turned back to his tent
With a trophy burdening his boyish arms,

With the lance that pierced the right side of Our Lord!
He's cured the king—he is himself the king
And priest who in his golden robe exalts

On bended knees the sacrosanct, adored
Chalice where the Pure Blood is shining,
—And the boys' cloistered voices fill the vaults.

[*Paul Verlaine*]

Poe's Tomb

As to Himself at last Eternity
Changes him, the Poet, with naked steel,
Challenges an age too tame to feel
How that strange voice proclaims Death's victory!

They, with a hydra's twitch, hearing the angel
Distill their *patois* to a purer sense,
Loudly denounce it—Witchcraft, drunk in the dense
Black brew of some dishonored spell.

From hostile earth and sullen cloud, O grief!
If to adorn the dazzling tomb of Poe
Imagination carves no bas-relief,

May this granite, from unknown disaster
Fallen here, at least its boundary show
To Blasphemy's black scattered flights hereafter.

[*Stéphane Mallarmé*]

Ecclesiastes

Saith the Preacher, Better a live mutt
Than a dead lion. All's smoke and shadow, save
Eating, drinking. And the world's in an old rut,
And the void of living fills the black grave.

From the summit of his tower, as on a bluff,
Facing the heavens through many a night long gone,
In silence, he lets his gaze alight far off
And muses darkly on his ivory throne.

Old lover of the sun, who'd thus lament,
Irrevocable death, too, is a lie.
Who leaps into it is engulfed, content!

But I, always, forever, appalled, hear rife
In the rapture and dread of immortality
The long roar of the everlasting life.

[*Leconte de Lisle*]

Lines Written near Linton, On Exmoor

By illness pent in lime-tree bower
And tossed upon the pains of sleep,
I gazed at lofty castle keep
With many a crenellated tower
On river bank—then, such a power
Poured through me, visionary, deep,
I seized my pen, in verse to keep
The revelation of that hour

—But who beats oar so hard on oarlock,
Importunately shakes my doorlock,
Stands on doorsill tugging forelock?
Salesperson, scholiast, or warlock
Dissolves my dream, his task, and the name
Of the wretched place from whence he came.

Evidence

"Money is a kind of poetry"—
Advice our great Assurer Stevens shared,
And who'd discount the statement undeclared,
That poetry's a kind of money?—since
The poem (whose returns, though nonfinancial,
Are active on the bourse of spirit) mints
All our common coin as transubstantial
Bonds, and puts our small change on the Real
Estate we most desire and hold tax-free.
Straight from the ticker with investor's zeal
Imagination banks on poetry:
Experience laid by accrues interest,
At what per cent we—whose security
Is balanced in such books—could scarce have guessed.

Philosophy of Composition

I'll flog you no more, old horse.
Old brain, weary, hoofed, thirsty,

You can't take me any farther. . . . So lie down
Here, and wait for my return.

I'll seize power without you.
I'll plunge on with no

Thought into the tangles
Of the hair of stars,

I'll get there without the tedium
Of turning passions

Into thinking, turning thoughts
To speech. Feelings will find me,

Words will come, the right ones,
Giving no thought, and taking none.

Addendum to *Daniel Hoffman:*
A COMPREHENSIVE BIBLIOGRAPHY

What author, scanning all his titles
But feels a twinge deep in his vitals?
See, here, and here, better he'd stayed
His pen, but published undismayed,
Though well he knew th'unbending Muse
Intolerant of all excuse
For an imperfect verse, and knows
That Truth demands no less of prose,
And yet the list, soon overlong,
Exhausts neither his speech nor song—
Go, little book, find reader, critic
As merciful as analytic
Who'll trace that visionary sphere
Hinted in shards and potsherds here.

ACKNOWLEDGMENTS

Several of these poems first appeared, some in slightly different form, in my
earlier volumes:

Broken Laws: "Ten Thousand Dreaming Seamen"
The City of Satisfactions: "The Arrival," "His Own Way,"
"Pin-Ball," and "O Sweet Woods"
The Center of Attention: "The Comanche," "The Sonnet"

Reprinted from the following volumes with the permission of Louisiana
State University Press:

Hang-Gliding from Helicon: "David's Folly," "Lines for Scott Nearing,"
"The Sacred Fount," "Scrolls from the Dead," and "That Morning"
Middens of the Tribe: (untitled) "Charley Hoope"
Darkening Water: "Philosophy," "Philosophy of Composition"
Beyond Silence: "A Resurrection," "Emblems," "In That High House,"
"Poe's Tomb," "The Sonnet," and "Violence"

Others first appeared in the following publications:

Boulevard: "Dr. Kilmer"
Literary Imagination: "The Disinherited"
Negative Capability: "Addendum to Daniel Hoffman: A Comprehensive
Bibliography"
New Hungarian Quarterly: "A Secret"
New Republic: "Who Done It?"
Poetry: "A Legacy"
The Sewanee Review: "Her Gift," "Old Age," and "Survivors"

And in these volumes:

New Selected Poems of Adam Mickiewicz, edited by Clark Mills
(Voyages Press, 1957): "At the Grave of Countess Potocka"
The X-Brand Anthology, edited by William Zaranka (Apple-wood
Books, 1981): "Lines Written near Linton, On Exmoor"

Sonnets not listed above appear here for the first time.

DANIEL HOFFMAN was Poet Laureate of the United States from 1973 to 1974. His first book, *An Armada of Thirty Whales*, was W. H. Auden's choice for the Yale Series of Younger Poets Award in 1954. His dozen later volumes include *Brotherly Love*, a finalist for the National Book Award and National Book Critics Circle Award; *Hang-Gliding from Helicon*; and *Darkening Water*. Hoffman was given the Arthur Rense Prize as "an exceptional poet" in 2005 by the American Academy of Arts and Letters. The best known of his critical studies is *Poe Poe Poe Poe Poe Poe Poe*, also a finalist for the National Book Award. Hoffman is the Felix E. Schelling Professor of English Emeritus at the University of Pennsylvania. He lives in Swarthmore, Pennsylvania, and Cape Rosier, Maine.